FAMILIAR AND FORGIVENESS

by
Katerina Vaughan Fretwell

"A child of the 1950s and 1960s, who grew up while eight family members fell dead before she reached the age of 25, Katerina Vaughan Fretwell (KVF) is a poet who has been to Hell and back, but has now landed well? *Familiar and Forgiveness* details that difficult, personal odyssey, a stark journey marked by the death of her father while she was yet a girl, and then her escape into booze, an abuse that rendered her a wreck of a mom, a depressed wife, and a drunken divorcée. What saved her, salvaged her, soothed her? *Poetry*—plus *Nature*. So, in Part I of this appealing, scarily honest, volume, KVF, tells us of her embrace of a cat, Cujo, who became, truly, the cat's meow, the cat's pyjamas. Here the poet produces lyrics about and *from* Cujo, who is her bewitching familiar—in the medieval, sense. This poetry is—*ahem*—catty in its wit, and then, in Part II, KVF reviews her life, her taking up of poetry and painting (as a visual artist) to emerge now as a healed and healthy elderessa (my coinage), glorying in her Celtic heritage (she is a descendant of 'metaphysical' poet Henry Vaughan) and, above all, in *Nature*. *Death* haunts her still, yes, for she has lost both Cujo and her second husband. But KVF offers us transcendent poetry—verses that uplift *Grief* unto the status of *Charity*. Who does she resemble? Oh, that's easy: Dylan Thomas."
—George Elliott Clarke, Author of *Canticles III (MMXXIII)* (Guernica Editions) & Parliamentary Poet Laureate of Canada (2016 & 17)

"No-one writes like Katerina Vaughan Fretwell, a poet at the top of her game. She invokes her illustrious name, Vaughan, not just for the 17ᵗʰ c. Welsh poet Henry, but for the little people summoned in her first section, Familiar. Here the cat's out of the bag and out of the box and yawling: this poetry is full of rollicking good humour, 'forensic without pause', with paws. Puns and pets run through the wide emotional gamut of experience of love and loss. Poems like 'in tune' must be

howled or at least read aloud! The play continues throughout the second section, Forgiveness, now in the Crone's more somber voice. These poems are blessings as Fretwell reflects on and releases her history, recognizing that she's no higher nor lower than other creatures, but just as 'elementally instrumental'."
—Penn Kemp, poet, playwright, performer

"Katerina Fretwell's Familiar and Forgiveness is clearly her best and most riveting volume of poetry to date. It combines wit and humour with amazing depths of perception about the recovery of the soul from trauma. The book unfolds in two richly interwoven sections. In 'Familiar' Cujo, the author's remarkable cat, is the speaker. In 'Forgiveness' the perspective of the author is primary, but Cujo accompanies 'Kat her Crone' through critical stages in her life. This well-crafted, autobiographical volume traces the difficulties of childhood, a descent into and recover from alcoholism, the death of a beloved partner, and reconnection with community. The rebirth of joy is wrought through a union of an art form and a new grounding in the natural world: 'Betrothed to poetry, art, and music,/ I wear humanity loose/ as a caftan (I hope),/ stretching 'Agape' from Selfie to the communal' ('Faerie Rings
Bless')."
—Susan McCaslin, poet and author of *Consider* (2023)

"Channelling John Berryman and Christina Rossetti, Fretwell sets the witches of Salem to rest in verses of exquisite music that could have, should have played in the mirror room of a baroque palace. A dazzling reclamation, reincarnation and revisitation of American and British spiritualist and lyrical traditions."
—Harold Rhenisch, author of *Landings: Poems from Iceland.*

"Katerina Fretwell's *Familiar and Forgiveness* explores the mythic and the mundane—with beautiful imagery, humour, empathy and gorgeous diction. Her unflinching speaker takes us on a journey and emerges as crone, eco-poet, social activist, and ultimately as phoenix rising victoriously from the ashes of alcoholism, 'coming alive/like Easter birth' into a 'world ...interconnected/fused by love.' This stunning collection of poetry ends with the joyous and well-deserved 'galaxy sized sober life/steeped' ... in the 'shimmering magnitude of gratitude'."

—Kate Marshall Flaherty, leader of Stillpoint, author of *Titch*

AOS PUBLISHING, 2024

AOS POETRY, 2024

ISBN: 978-1-990496-60-8

Cover Design: Chanelle Poupart
Painting Serpentine Renewal by Katerina Vaughan Fretwell

Visit AOS Publishing's website:
www.aospublishing.com

Table of Contents

Dedication:

to all cat lovers, medicine men and women,
and impassioned forest walkers. Sinuous, succouring, insurgent.

SECTION ONE:
FAMILIAR

Cujo Herself Speaks:

(for Patti who dreamed that Cujo scrawled Familiar)

C'est moi, la grande chatte, a claw-eyed calico poet
misnamed Cujo. Bewitchingly Familiar to Kat my Crone,

and woodsy boon to her Celtic credit
that the life force propels all beings.

I landed with Kat because her daughter hoped
to forestall a neighbour's heart attack!

All I did was tromp on the woman's veggie plot,
edgy on a squirrel's trail, my breath tickling its tail.

I begrudge the transplant, and yet
chez Fretwell, I track five whole acres

worth of land to domesticate, mice to scarf ...
About my misname?

Male calicoes are rare, frail, and
often sterile. Ha! We'll see about that!

I'm always willing to hold up my end!
Friend ....

Encrypt Me Egyptian

O joie de vivre, Crone's prone to slavery:
I saunter to my bowl; servile, she'll follow,

and sit tail-wrapped, an Egyptian Goddess,
like the carved tulip-wood feline

rapt at her hearth. Or I arch like the Great
Goddess Nut bowing the Nile sky.

Antediluvian priests deified me as Bast, the catty
aspect of Nut. Egypt's feral felines,

still sacrosanct, are proffered octopus
by folk and Pharaohs. Reality resumes:

Kat pulls the tab on Fancy Food,
chops a beggars' banquet into nuggets

I sniff, then ignore, mincing to the front door.
Crone cathecizes: Food? Outside? *Simpleton.*

Here's the Scoop, I'm a Thinker

Crone and I zip to our *toilettes*. My House of Litter's
scooped nightly, so I alight upon cleanliness *toujours.*

Like Crone, I croon for slumber, yet lay awake –
as Eco-cat: masticating poems, journals,

brown bags, foil-wrap; as Enviro-cat:
Reduce, Recycle, Regurgitate.

*

Bestowed upon me, a host of golden catnip
for my gifted three Rs (see above). So there,

dear Willy Wordsworth, your golden daffodils
cloud my brain – too mundane for my taste-buds.

My gravelly growl's a philosopher's
pebble-in-mouth irritated oration.

Re: Creativity, I Create, Too!

My mistress obsesses over each brush-stroked
canvas-study, the better to vet her errors.

She squirts Ultramarine onto her palette,
flings two dabs (sighs, Enough) then sprays

acrylic blobs for re-use, shrouds them in foil-wrap,
as refrigerator–yummy as her sonnets and sestinas.

*

Crone's fear of erring is a mere red-herring
for the self-doubting blues. She needs a boost

from Bast and me: We Great Goddess emblems
blast her pussy-footing with our strut and stride!

*

Once I sat on her art-slash-dining-table
My dear striped tail flipped into the Titanium White.

Mistress then gazed at Familiar painting #5,
saw my paw prints made it come alive!

No copycat,
just the catty original!

Sleeping Solo, Sigh

Widow Crone's a monk on her twin-size bed.
Coucher avec moi, comme on dit en franglais?

It's hard stretching on that narrow surface.
My preferred spot targets her crotch,

that she claims maims her bladder control.
Kicked off, I curl on the queen-size bed

in the open-concept-bedroom, which, she opines,
jumbles her slumber with light and noise.

She forbids Don Juan in her habitat.
What a Kattitude! Hie me to a cattery!

O long-haired Lotharios, we'll breed flattery
till Crone's prone to sharing her cot *avec moi.*

Eroticat, I Am

Hey, I'm spayed, but I do spray and splay
for the intact tabby a purr away.

La vie d'amour among the cattails is divine,
but never, never cross that line:

the tabby usurped MY porch at MY door.
At least Kat yelled: Scat. I'm floored –

my late master dubbed my campy
spread legs and exposed belly – vampy:

Cujo's cheesecake pose. I'm a fashion hawk:
regarde moi strolling a Paris catwalk.

I bare my privates as Cat Goddess Bast's prime fan –
imparting elan earns me a salmon repast.

I 'tomcat' because I don't pussyfoot around:
I'm like Fritz, never-on-the-fritz, and never housebound.

My Black Bird Tutorial

Wallace Stevens versed "Thirteen Ways of Looking
at a Blackbird". Dummy, there's only one way:

tilted into my tummy! I teach Crone
biology, presenting rodent parts:

kidneys and heart on her blue welcome mat,
no preservative required – how hard is that?

I chomp blackbird pie and vole guacamole. That,
dear Wallace Stevens, is a performance poem,

to beat out all. I post what I maul
in verses of severed head and/or tail!

Verse also spells out <u>sever,</u> eh?
My poesy is forensic without pause ...

Crone's Catharsis, My Verse

Crone cashes her Sobey's points for free food:
scarfs oysters and lobster for Valentine's.

Pour moi? Rien. Then she parades her late mate's
faves on piano. What devoted caterwauling!

Next, glued to her laptop, she unglues stuck-together poems,
ignoring *moi* under her desk, bereft, as if also bereaved.

I claw her sweats, scare her up for a stroll
to my bowl. See, I, too, perfect rhyme.

Ah, such a briny catnip just for me?
You're mellowing, O mistress mine!

If I were an Ocean-loving Cat

I dream myself a Maritime cat
noshing fresh-killed fish. But, less romantically,
we're foraging in Ontario, heaven of scavengers.

Hands full filleting blackberry bushes,
Crone can't swat a homing-in mosquito.
Former Herring-Choker, she recalls

Solomon Gundy's pickled herring
and the Bay of Fundy's righteous, hydraulic-lifted wall,
highest haul of tides in the world.

She pines for Five Fishermen fine dining.
In Crone and I troop with bibs for chowder,
bobbing for apple-pan-dowdy.

Come again; in line for brine?
Blimey, I'm down the hold –
I'll catch cold in the clammy cargo!

O drawn butter and bouillabaisse –
this succulent seafood feast is dreamed to the tune
of the pesky skeeter buzzing Kat's ear.

My Proven Adorable Angle

Cradling me, Crone heels to her scale,
expounds: Yay, you weigh eight pounds!

Eight in numerology pronounces power.
While Crone records my gain, I munch on

ces poèmes, par moi, de moi,
inspiring her thundering dander.

I lower my eyes in a fail-safe angle,
avert swats, or worse, for chewing up said bespoke verse.

Draped cross her writing table, I flash amber-
greens in her face. She sighs, rises, feeds,

and frees me outdoors. I proceed,
marking my turf with hurled poetry –

morphed papier-machee marvels;
add sculptor to my resume, Rodin –

And no paper tiger am I,
but catty to ham-fisted scribble –

So pleased to dig in my claws!

I'm Also Capsized

Time to mention my nemesis, Psyche,
a Persian/Himalayan, ship's cat clone,

loving all things fishy, already here
upon my transplant to Kat's. So, I gave Psyche

a wide berth, no copycat mariner, I'll nosh
Fancy fine-finned sea fare, but, shudder, not ship rats.

I prefer a catamaran, anyway!
(Let rats fatten, slipped loose aboard cruise ships!)

When Psyche shipped out, Jack claimed
even the vet cried tear-sunk galleons. But now,

no contest: I'm Alpha Cat, best in showboat,
yeah, I know, also the only feline present ...

Oy, my master's four a.m. final ship-ahoy –
I endure widowed Crone's anchoring-cuddles.

My Catechism for Raising Humans 101

The cat's out of the bag: a feline text
for subduing and training a human:

> Withhold praise till she's your smitten slave.
> Stifle hunger 'till she sets down your fave.
>
> To flee a kick at the cat down to the floor
> don't jump on her bed 'till after she snores.
>
> Shred her poems to jolt her from the Zone –
> writing oms to a cat's-meow, fish-stew Cornpone.
>
> Witness her snowshoe entry and exit. She'll grin
> at your focus on her, not your chinny-chin-chin.
>
> Make her open the front and then the back-door
> for the shortcut through the house; this, I adore.
>
> Enter your litter *toute-de-suite* after she cleans it.
> Keen like a cat on a hot tin roof and mean it –
>
> whenever pads close a neighbour's – a capella:
> howling and growling pit-bull dubbed Bella.

Let's Paint-a-Kat

This time I played scarce – Cheshire-ing
from Crone's basement-into-gallery

makeover. After painting the walls white,
she fanny-walked, colouring the floor grey,

but marred the whitewashed walls
with grey splats.

A sucking sound erupted
during her derriere-sweep.

Grunting upright to oust the kinks,
fingering her seat, grey paint-patties

dotting her sweatpants, she yelped:
"Widowhood sucks!" Even my whiskers vamoosed!

After all, I'm happy to 'tomcat' about –
letting puritans and eunuchs pout!

Parting is Such...

... a time for fussy mush – Crone airs her black-
bag, cheating *moi:* no food on MY time-track.

Roger, my late master's best bud, is A-OK,
but his gas-gulping truck alights but once a day –

I wolfed down four tins. But I undid Crone:
nine hours after her return, I waltzed home.

When I darkened the door, she hugged my fur flat.
This hot grief flatters me: I'm her Welcome Mat.

SECTION TWO:
FORGIVENESS

I Embrace My Celtic Nature

Celtic heritage, I entreat you,
heft my non-mellow spirit,

dealing with death, debts, and driving demerits –
rising ire at the dire world and foul-weather climates.

My maternal forebears were Saxons,
paternal, Celts, all but English –

no surprise they staged *up*risings –
fair play galvanizing their flinty genes.

Mystic forebear Henry Vaughan believed the body
healed itself, shunned mercury and leeching cures ...

[Would neither self-poison
nor let out his blood.]

*

Hugging my fave hemlock sugars my raves,
rants bantering about the slanted wheel of fortune.

Forested widow, I heed critters' creeds;
sprucing my path with pining oracles –

butterfly alights: colour up your life;
toad jumps out: changes are afoot.

I'm content with the detente instanced
by my late mate's blatant screens.

My shadow/blighted side welcomes
the night's pixelated, silver-dappled dark

and airs my flaws in bedtime checklists,
amends to make, doled out in dreams.

Wilderness Chorale

In my forest hermitage, past my cat Cujo's trail –
       my lungs exhale woodland recitative
in tongues, sung by ancient, adept Celts.

No longer sprayed with chemicals
       to kill spruce bud-worm, conifers
breathe relief, now also spared from Yuletide-axe.

During the Fall hunt, a black squirrel,
       upon sighting a sighting rifle, flees,
astutely hides on the red oak's unseen side.

When I snowshoe, the critters
       SOS: clicks, caws and cackles.
Ah, I inhale their creaking medley

that just is, no treble, bass, time, or key.
       I belong to this blissful song,
marvel at the beech buds aglow on snow –

gracefully detached, convinced I'm not
       higher or lower than the squirrels
but simply as elementally instrumental!

Earth Care

Womb and tomb of all, Earth blessings pour
        on all lifeforms and lifespans,
from grunted worms to unbound wingspans.

But warmongers bloody and shudder Earth,
spray poisons, release toxins, to taint
biology with morbidity,

*

or fake or make insurgent rain
to stretch or scratch crops;
or else they dam up water damnably.

*

When military-brass lead poisons the Earth
with bullets, with depleted uranium,
the Earth's cancer maddens the climate.

*

Ah, Cujo and I rake earth's twitching skin,
        sniff the blooms and revere
leaf-art and trillium-quilt designs.

In her wetlands, the tree-frogs chorus,
        and bullfrogs gronk hello.
Cujo and I step lighter, breathe in

the truffle-soil smell of soil and company
        coming to life,
speaking to my pen, brush, and voice.

Accentuate Avalon

In King Arthur's Avalon, Morgaine Le Fey
tinctured potions to medicine sinners and critters.

Celts chatted in Gaelic with Bird-Woman
before Babel spooked we humans into acting

as if we're not even animals,
so we eschew natural cures – for test-tube toxins.

Once, hunters blessed the hunted, smoked, and salted
for the season of no stags or surplus fat.

Real-time chats, tea-talk and birdsong
have lost out to inane e-talk and twitter-twit-tweet.

But, in Avalon, every bard was Orpheus,
or Dr. Doolittle. And still we are ... If we're in tune ....

Spirit Dancers Dream Big

Blithe and lithe, the wee folk, elves and faeries
dance from dawn to dusk, 'big up' birds and berries.

Here, not here, they pan the pecking order,
tricking the tyrant, so the lowly raid the larder,

helped by Robin Hood and Maid Marian.
How they jitterbug away jitters antiquarian.

I two-step out of grudges, sensing the wee folk
in ringed-fields: portals in the whirling air.

The Welsh Goddess, Cerridwen, grins and spins
revolutions. Braving change, though strangely petite,

I dream of their sleights. My patronymic
Vaughan means Little People.

But there's nothing alight
about how we carry on –

And nothing petty about our heights –
always Olympian, always Aquarian.

Earth Lungs

Fashioned into crosses and stakes, trees receive
heretics' last gasp by those nailing their land;

pressed into pages, hardwoods spread real and fake news,
praising or panning seekers and suppressors,

[rightly or wrongly,
colourfully or black-and-white plain,]

Carved into pulpit, podium, or platform,
they prop up preacher, prof, or politico;

cross-sectioned, the ringed boles record
human warfare or weather cataclysms.

Trees shade the sun, flush the air,
yield homes, fire, and medicine.

So, down with saw, axe, and lumberjacks!
Off with their headspace, not our world's green canopy!

Replace boardrooms with head-shops and co-ops.
Replace limos with donkey carts – or tumbrels!

Entanglement

Two distinct but entangled atoms join –
a happy Kenyan bee and a grinning Dane.
This inter-linkage whirls in sync,

reflecting the Elizabethan belief
that the world is interconnected –
fused by love.

Now scientists know how atoms
catapult and catalyze this connection, electrons
partying in an energy swap.

And atoms explain the results of chanters
throwing their oms into the airwaves:
entice enough of them and behold –
crime and divorce rates fall.

Teamwork outshines the fickle:
"You're number one!"
Best/worst comparisons knock out
any hard-won equilibrium.

A woods walk, amid bramble
and brush, bush and tangle,
I see light caught up in each path I amble,
I see light figuring out each angle.

Serpentine Renewal

After tonguing my tart retorts
or forking tallied flaws –
I slough my old modes
like a snake's shed persona.

Even the avid mouser, Cujo,
prefers to play rather than slay.

The Eden-myth Scribes demoted
serpent to tempter, phallus –
projecting their stumbles onto the reptile,
a humble, ground-level viewer, eating dust.

But, no how-to books are required –
rebirth is hardwired into snake's DNA.

Minoan Crete adored the ancestral
Snake Goddess, who presided over
women as well as men
dancing on the backs of bulls,
symbolizing agile, bullish governance –

before the marauding Dorians
and a tidal wave buried Crete,
before the Scribes vilified the species,
claiming a snake led Eve astray.

My serpentine takeaway:
as Crone, I can atone, ply on
a new bodysuit!

Numbers Wield Power

Ancient Celts revered the number Three:
new moon, till; half moon, sow; full moon, reap,
young, maiden; middle-age, matron; old age, crone –
natural cycles taught options and outcomes.

Then electricity faked daylight, skewed the cycles,
but scientists still honoured intuition –
dreamed of DNA as a double helix:
two sacred spirals entwined.

Now numbers shrink to zeros and ones:
these bits and bytes bind humankind
into the triple World Wide Web
and program the pixels
to be on call twenty-four/seven.

Relayed speech can unite humans:
in the Arab Spring, cellphones tweeted
huge meet-and-greets,
dialed up demos for democracy.

But *1984's* the new 911,
or maybe even 9 – 11,
if tyrants can control all info.

Hold on to handwriting
as the old-new-sedition,

best hold out *via* handwriting
as the neo-traditional sedition.

Faerie Rings Bless

I smile, slide into oneness
        stars aligned
                harmony refined –
graceful as sketching pebble posies on a lake.
Fear, awe and joy – through Faerie –
ring cycles, biblical tribal links.

Nation
        neighbourhood
                and street shrink
into a Google-eyed, shop window.

Fear, awe and joy, these rings
        hover over loners' bare ring-finger ache
for endorsement on LinkedIn.

Betrothed to poetry, art, and music,
        I wear humanity loose
                as a caftan (I hope),
stretching "Agape" from Selfie to the communal:

Platonic love baked in a friendship cake
gifts all-purpose gratitude.
        When I am thankful –
its altitude lifts me free of fear.

Go tabann: suddenly saplings are greener;
        parkas, warmer; defects, accepted;
love of self and love on the net
                in the ring cycle of the web
make magic possible –
even for riding bucking Valkyries ....

Lower World Holds Power

On my woods-walks, flattened pine's naked roots
        trowel a snowed-in cave.

Through this forest leeway, my ego courts
        the foxy aphorisms of strategic creatures:

Breathe, keep still, Crone, envision
        a Jules Verne voyage spelunking your core:

Where spiders spin Sibelius "Fantasias,"
        and beavers gnaw on a vernal Nautilus (a log).

Where moles dream humans humming
        over dish-washing soap blooms.

Where bats sashay to Virginia Reels,
        and salamanders sway to Sarabands.

Where taproots speak in tongues,
        and night-crawlers splice all broken souls,

it is possible to heal broken spirits:
I've witnessed soused losers' Twelve-Step progression

out of Barleycorn's Bar, Mordor's Cave, Dante's Inferno.
I am One with snow fleas and grizzlies, frizzly with snow.

Pre-hominids Weren't Primitive

Before the stained glass allegories, mosaic myths,
and upthrust spires, sacred wells beamed me back:

Where Druids were truant – nature as is – before
stupid homo sapiens toyed with dubious alloys.

Where first-farmers preserved seedlings –
heartier than mono-crops monotonously tasteless and greed-
priced seeds.

Where in 5000 BCE – bed-fellows
in bat-pooped forts, named and tamed the whole cosmos –

now IT wizards slouch ancient apelike shoulders –
over screens and scopes, each a patent of its parent.

Now too slack for Early Celtic's rough living,
I still culture Big Bang bacteria:

conjure the germs that sprout forth wheat;
dread the unleashing of germ warfare.

Georgian White Pine Dances

Munching blueberries near Dinner Lake,
I climb a Georgian White Pine,

press my ear to the osmotic chute,
hear syrup-pulse flow up and down.

Crickets, nature's town-criers, abrade their legs;
red oaks creak in the deke-ing wind.

Aflame, I steep large brushes
into cadmium and indigo.

My spirit paints itself – like the old Celts
leaping over ritual bonfires, or Big

Lonely Doug rocking in a clear-cut
daubing the sky in gratitude to Dennis Cronin.

Wowed by Fall's cadmium, why can't people see
trees love us? We'd hear

Big Lonely Doug mourn for fallen kin –
The dead leaves? The fading notes ...

as I lament felled family, hugging
my Crying Hemlock encircled by mate's ashes.

His uprooting roots me
where I'm otherwise uprooted.

Auguries

Like Tarot, Celtic cards divine
a problem's sources and solutions –

each card's image and placement gets deciphered
in the companion book.

Rejected submissions prompted me
to seek artistic direction.

Fighting Horses card landed on the spot
showing my mind's a maelstrom

trying to impress the genius of my late mother,
trying to be clever with a disengaged heart.

But how do I retrace expectancy,
find praiseworthy flesh my own flesh damns?

How do I avert worry of sadness, Grief?
Oh the lone intellect's a stubborn stench!

Primitive Art Can Be Hip

Maud Lewis's childlike – but pictorial – flat planes
speak to my abstract art Many Paths –

> its ragged blotches and Hieronymus Bosch byways
> mimic a toddler's zigzag s/crawl.

There's a place for brush-stroked
stop-start, straight-curved, grid-lines

> looking like ship-shape sea-lanes, not smoggy traffic
> jams.
> Bridged splotches, even flops, reap a chimp's prize

or a cat's-pyjamas Picasso – after 10,000 practised hours.
I pave over lame brush-strokes

> with opaque acrylics. Celtic cards tell:
> memorize the map, then hit the thicket –

abstraction's uncharted byways foretell
where soul must dwell – oceanic and open –   ·

in the pools of a Dali-esque melting,
Time curving all codified rigidity.

Gabriel Is My Virgil

Healing in-house in Aurora included
a meditation to glean one's spirit-guide,
and then an outdoor treasure hunt
for seekers to follow our instincts
over the grounds to see what called us
to homing in, dig up to dig in.

My senses communed with cattails,
climbed the clouds,
and accessed Archangel Gabriel,
a Virgil steering me to self-love's heaven.

I grinned on sunlit snowbanks,
startling my heart into its mirror blaze.

Shedding ego's doomed comparisons,
I embraced Being differently –
the skittish balance
between we and thee

(what we call the dance
of give and get).

Cards Warn Me

Celtic Book of the Dead

This illustrated book demystifies
each card's picture and placement.

I ask the cards what stymies Art? Politics!
Widowed, I collected death, ire, and traffic tickets.

Silver Net flutters: Becalmed on a balmy sea,
strain out the mind-fog that clogs your joy.

Songbirds trill: Stop twittering negatives.
Hear your pipes, leave gloomy grooves.

Raptor descants: Wing words outward,
flow into the lava-heat of you here.

But my mind first balks – feels damn fine to leap lofty
onto a pulpit firing off the world's faults

in didactic art and poems. On an updraft,
I enrol in driver's ed, clear debts and demerits.

Deplore the professors on one side,
and defang the police on the other.

Cards Call Oceanic

Tarot-diviners, Celtic cards
portray me as Queen of the Castle:

But I squirmed during sermons and bolted
from Betters in correction mode ...

*

The seventh wave grinds pride
into grimy crab trails.

I rise wiser, 'till the next breaker
smacks my hubris. Strolling the Golden

Mean, I dive into the combers,
content to be merely Part Of.

Heir to the family cravings,
but not the family genius,

I gratefully surf the sunlit sea
substance-free for over four decades

soaring above
their alcoholic moat,

ferocious with piranha,
craving to have at brains.

I, Crone, Admire Refitted Lost Souls

Long before head doctors, shamans
healed many-people-in-one

called alters or soul parts.
Some alters sound, look, hear,

and write differently and distinctly –
than the head-ego who blocks off these parts

to survive particular times
and places of torture.

*

Like protein knitting fractured bones whole –
refitted, patients sleep cat-sound. Each found soul.

Gabriel Glued Me Whole

In Aurora, tending our accursed traumas,
we seekers hand to scratch ten angry pages daily.

My spirit-guide, the Archangel Gabriel,
shape-shifted my upheld Bic into a healing athame.

Through penning hate letters to my parents,
I assumed their ills – scapegoating my genius.

Mom's solitary confinement in books
and Dad's mama's boy, pantywaist youth.

Exhuming their pain, I found Mom's angst,
doctored by books, so she cringed backstage in siblings' dramas;

and I found Dad's home-schooled delusion,
all these snaps portraying him as his mama's hubby.

Parental taunts now made sense:

Anagnorisis informed my diagnosis.
Of course, they saw me as an "arty flake."

Self-enforced was my salvaging:
To pen and paint, my stockpiled bile finally

drawn off as ink, as oils, as watercolours.
All outrage posted to pastel or poured into poetry.

I Defused Night Terrors

(I, Crone, as Child, Woman)

After Daddy fatally choked on Christmas turkey and Scotch,
too young to remember that defining day,
but absorbing the panic,
I lulled myself to sleep with a game,
if I counted to ninety-nine,
loved ones would live that long.

Eight dead by my twenty-fifth birthday,
I drank daily for twelve years
to omit the void, to forget the fear.

Night Terrors drenched me twice
in one night with the exact same dream:
Daddy yanked toddler me screaming
into the unlit basement.

The doctor assigned after my age-thirty insanity alert,
drugged me against pulsating bile.
The last beau of my debauched 1970s
pierced my post-session desolation.
I fired the doc, plugged the jug,
and dreamed lucid the Night Fiends' demise.

Now, at last, my big fat gleaming grin
stuns all Terrors into mundane bogeymen.

Hemlocks as Health

I breathe hemlocks in, hemlocks breathe in me.
Their soul language chides me: Not apologizing
for that deep wrong now lumped in my gut and throat.
I know, I know! A sudden shadow scuds.
I recall the distressed and plundered nest
that resounds with my daughter's unheard cries.
Snowshoes fly, I gasp, *What have I done!*
I write my fledgling, who responds with love.

Bough-perched, a songbird unlocks arias.

Beeches Quicken

Beech-sienna buds
        shimmy auras on white:
                silver outlines pulsate on
                winter's ivory wool-duvet
        floored to outdoor stairs
widow's step-landing.

They glow knowing,
        to urge me out, lift
                shovelling troubles
                through record snow-
        fall, cold snap, pray
and display red flags

for my defrost. Phero-
        mones yawn, stretch
                post-three year grief.
                Here beeches leaf
        despite raging blight.
Their veins divest light

to my trance-synoptic
        dance. Colour-starved,
                I lift snowshoes
                racing to unfurl joy.
        Dream-catchers fetch
hope, project palette wheels of perception.

Mine, theirs: pests,
        logging, cloud-seeds,
                skidoos' gassy trails,
                clear-cut   saplings.

        I love my beeches,
I beach in their flurried, light-rich flutters.

2016

Giant Fireflies, Skidoos Flicker

Winter fireflies fly trails
that flare and fade,
the darkness backdrops
their meteor-dazzling run.

This fleeting run answering why
I feel secure: their trails
actually stop those who covet
this land to pave it.

Seeing Skidoos fly
nightly over the trails
like disembodied meteors
from the dark and driven shore,
my transient running complaints drop.

My vision lit, off rail,
their shadowy run resembles
lightning's cry, a jagged pop.

A pin could drop:
this chiaroscuro is surely
a drama on the fly –
taillights, back-lit
on the northbound run,
light less trails

than headlights on the southbound trails.
Snowmobiles knock off abominable snowmen,
lighting up their paleface greed,
then lancing them with fly-by-night light,
as they go poof – take a powder.

Oomph!

Forests Supported Crone

(as Child and Crone)

I skipped through the Sunapee woods,
from cabin to lake, child and teen years soothed:
Stravinsky's "Firebird Suite" mirrored my kin's
discordant keys: who'd die drunk next?

My young chords unmoored, I felt atonal
beside the yacht club's operatic preppies,
so I regressed: morphing moss into faerie gardens,
finding harmony in timeless nature.

Many forest revels later, my mate and I
visited the Welsh Brecon Beacons, the home
of ancestral bard Henry Vaughan, Celtic spawn,
at last the tonic!

Now, in a forest larger than that by Vaughan's
Scethrog cottage, at the hemlock stand near
sweet home, Seguin, Ontario, I scat

the jazzy notes of my late beloved aunt,
artist, dancer, and cat lover, who carved
a feline out of tulip-wood that guards my hearth,

affirming the path that chose me – Familiar,
Cujo, and Celtic lore, my woodland wealth.
Firebird morphed into Phoenix.

Chopin's Opus 53 Blessing

On my Northern Europe and Russian Tour
in 2015, at the Chopin Warsaw Park,
I pushed the special bench's button
and presto: "Opus 53
Polonaise" plunged me into yearning,

echoing my classics immersion
in childhood. "53" elevated the jams:
with me or my uncle on piano,
cousin on guitar, tone-deaf mom
drumming pots, and aunt twirling *en pointe.*

Resounding worldwide, Opus 53 arched
over the Atlantic to the Chopin master,
Janina Fialkowska's finessing fingers,
massaging the Yamaha Grand
at the Bay's Festival of the Sound.

And my joints – rejuvenated – jump,
and gone loved ones return, spry in fantasies.

Irvington Woods Ballasted Me

(as Child, Teen, Late Teen)

In postwar New York, as a Child, I sprinted through
the Irvington woods, to save my fave
gronking bullfrog from pre-fab housing.

Puffing Cools and soaping curse words
on the shiny panes, I hid with partners
in crime each time a cop rolled past.

*

Fatherless at two, no witness to coupling's
cozy, dark, or coping secrets, as a naive Teen
I cuddled my cat, regressed to dressing dolls,

roaming the tall grasses and co-reading
Gone With The Wind and *Little Women*
with my gal-pal in foster-care.

Hibernating in hemlock stands
after each fizzled crush, I feared
boys – a strange and invasive species.

*

Some were orangutans posed as Baptists;
others were ex-sailors learning to crawl on land;
a few were gangsters in debonair duds.

At Acadia, first co-ed place since grade school,
I met boys right rowdy, not just spruced-up for dates
or posted on pedestals as exotic wallets.

Swapping class notes and sweating at swim meets,
as a Late Teen, I kissed my favourite date,
our hearts honking like courting frogs.

Ochre Epiphanies

Painting soul   my lifelong goal: homing strokes
to land on   a personality pilgrimage.   Full values

browns to beige with blue hints   hone my tone.
No portraitist's golden palette   palatable marks

my hazel eyes peer out   from sombre ground
contrary to culture's   beatified Youth.

Wisdom scumbled   from scored brownouts
restores light   ochre epiphanies.

Beauty accrues   from stark contrasts
desperation contours   character.

Beyond mascara wand   or Botox tuck
crone-hood fetes   each silvered strand.

Embodied being   palate-knifed grounded
multi-valued under-painting: behold I Am

this moment   my gaze   dwells in yours.
One life   one plane   singular   many-faceted Soul.

What is self: times   remembered   sobbed   giggled.
In rendering myself   flaws blooms all   I am painting you.

Blow Cold Many Moons

The air chills for forty sub-zero days
and six minus-forty nights –
the thermostat's the new wheel of fortune.
I cave in flannel-thermals,

and resemble a demented mole. My wool
nose-warmer prevents the ice
from sculpting my snout. Outdoors,
I burrow in balaclava

and North Face strata. Unlike "American Dream",
Canada's lives a half-year shelf-life –
sunlight on sabbatical. And yet ...

*

The Arctic's melting thrice as fast
as science foretold, proclaims the Nobel
nominee, Sheila Watt-Cloutier.

All dwellers, ice floes and permafrost
are climate canaries – Inuit and Dene
now seared and singed, bake like Alaska.

Cloning their earth-reverence is our only hope:
first broadcast before being censored, the UN
watchdog claimed: doomed earth-life is worth grief.

Ironwood's Chi, Fleeting Gift

Half-way in, the ironwood reveals its chi –
bonding is foremost in this February freeze.
Minutes later, a silver-tinged blue-band
shimmies two feet from the ironwood bole,
luminous heartbeat hopscotching
left to right. [I thank this tree, chant:
Preserve this tree, forest and planet.]

Wintergreen season is berry-red and snow-free –
leeks are gone to glory, trillium, not yet pink,
no black-flies swarm, but there's no snow to reflect
the tree's life force. Bereft, I still honour the invisible chi.
Does my pride expect a select light show:
entranced and triple-hued like the Northern Lights?
The chi needs no witness, my fealty is ever green.

Gumption Can't Suppress Arctic Breath

Honouring the Samhain/Halloween custom,
I write down one of my defects to burn off
in the symbolic cauldron, as dark trumps light.

The six minus-forty nights top Ripley's Record.
Six months, seemingly subnivean, can't outrank
the June snow in Eighteen-Sixteen: greenhorns starved.

No partner blast-furnaces my bed,
igloo-cold creeps under my gumption:
ices the conduit, stops the flow.

*

Abruptly, I lean into my fecund breeze,
trails and lawns slough their parkas.
The frigid pipe clears its throat, clinks to cut-time.

Peepers out-sing the Vienna Boys Choir,
pipe-in the once sleeping, now-spooning,
Corn God and Goddess – mentors

mooning round the Maypole, sowing the Three
Sisters: maize, squash, and beans. Snow runnels
off the Shield, stunning all my self-pity.

2014

Avian Choristers Tremolo

Cujo and I loiter on the flowered porch,
twilight melds into a one-note Kelly-green,
the sleepy sun marks time over the treetops,

conducting avian choristers:
finches, nuthatches, warblers, and redpolls ...
fine-tuning gloaming lullabies.

Nest reduced, fledgling fledged, mate deceased –
serenity jolts me, seventy-plus,
suddenly released from the He-She of house-holding.

A goitre-pressed low tenor, I warble,
strain, and stretch to famous choral works
in the Riversong Choir, my ego dubbed

over and out. The trilling nightfall
thrills Cujo and reassures me.
Nightingale descants, over and out.

My Shamanic Session for Crone; My Response

Shifted prone, quilted, shut-eyed, Crone
        sensed my stones opening her chakras.
                As a Sin Eater, I spat out her flaws,

        but I glossed over the life details
      that steered her here and passed up
the time to retrieve her split-off parts.

I served her spiced chamomile tea.
      Then Crone shipped out, never
           homing to my harbour again.

*

Sleepless, my huge sluice flooded,
      I steamed home pit stop by pit stop,
          no split-off parts safe-harboured.

        Anchored by Goddess through the ship's
      rat-hold of drink, I'm liberated forty years
past kin's deaths, my divorce and dereliction.

I honour this four-decade-old path.
      My driven-steerage becalmed, I peel
        off paranoia and hug my albatross,

        loving kith, kin, and pilgrims;
      slow-sail by slow-sail, my quirks
and quarks wink: I'm steeped in love.

Courting Sleep

Sleep is the dark again in a new form
that wraps the body tighter and in it dreams
are a vast swarming world, a little town and farm
long bygone set in a legend in flower.
A.F. Moritz, *Sequence*, 115.

Courting sleep is a leap between worlds,
each shut-eye, a tiny death.
Mom's mantra, Never go to bed
on a quarrel, billowing
in my dreams.
I slumber against the norm –
the rise-and-shiners that kiss
the swelling sun.
Moonlight blesses me. I'm reborn –
sleep is the dark again in a new form.

Parental Christmas Eve discord
shadowed Daddy's death
on Jesus's birthday.
Mom never revealed her fateful words –
still I conjoined sleep-fight-death
in our mortal stream.
I practised mentally
my counting game to drift off –
trusting its diversionary theme
that wraps the body tighter, and in it dreams

a psychic clearinghouse
of childhood rhymes.
"If I should die before I wake .... "
"Lost and gone forever,
O my darling Clementine" – released grief
before I came to lifelong harm.
In our daycare barn, stunned silent
yet concerned, urging me to sing our loss
in "Clementine," Mom became a wise schoolmarm.
A vast swarming world, a little town and farm

planted in me, the dread of bedtime's
crossing into nocturnal death –
'till resolved through pivotal dreams,
a lucid and vivid day-glow sheen.
I decipher what works, leave the rest –
the moon's still my bloom of the hour,
sleeping-in exalts my day.
That Long Island dilettante farm –
recalls the glory of its magnolia bower
long bygone set in a legend in flower.

Interment

we're mostly only powder /from the dust /of teeth and bones
John B. Lee, *The Full Measure,* "Remains," 37.

Weeping into the woods, from your ashes
I sculpted a crown around my Crying Hemlock,
your white bone-bits blending on the piney-ground,
my woods chapel where I mourned your slow slippage,
dementia robbing us of Jack, bit by bit.

Before your cancer and after your angina,
and diabetes death knells, we recounted last dreams.
You pined for burial over the Atlantic
where we met and you floated thirty naval years.
But after you died, I couldn't afford the sea.

I poured the rest of your ash into the Bay, hoping
they'd scoot from Parry Sound to your desired site.
Then something uncanny overrode my regrets
and recalled the special roses you nurtured:
your ashes, just below the water's surface,

floated a six-petalled, pale Rugosa Rose ....

(Late husband, Jack Fretwell, 1937-2013.)

Celtic Coda

Empty yourself and let the universe fill you.
Yogi Ginger Tea quote.

This dream-poem floats on low dose codeine
hacking my constant, clear-cut hacking.

I contracted this on a rainbow-lit eve –
colours' omen: I'm not Hades-bound yet?

Empty myself for what? The prism's premise:
Slow down. Whooping cough clears my cot –

my cat, jumping off, ogles my dream Raven:
Seer or Meal? Moonlight dances bright sprites

on my overgrown lawn, while the whole cosmos
cavorts – Trickster arrives via Vicks Vapours,

tea and soulful soup, attuned to this Celtic June.
Hello priestess, Solstice mischief – all lift up

the cone of power, be merry and well:
Cujo and I osmose unquestionable joy.

Pagans Also Baptize

Baptisms whistle in clover. I pick
thirteen blackberries singing in falsetto,
and recall the Maritime Jack-in-the-Pulpit.

Religion hymns through the trees, but I too
steward tree stands and creeks, flowing
nobly, as Cardinal loftily observes.

Blackberries, at home in thorns, preside over
the tryouts for the grasshopper chorus.
The congregation shrinks and the bullfrog mutes –

his flexible spats are too gluey for wooing.
Thorns crown Vipers Buglos – we pagan spirits
anoint snapdragons and the Three Sisters.

A sunlit thistle counterpoints the jiggling
jewel-weed – and a praying mantis jumps
over the anthills seeking the Afterlife.

Celtic Wisdom Chants

I open my arms and I am the forest.

Mystery lands in sunsets.

A maze amazes me, the circles are encircled.

I open my third eye into the "I" of every storm.

Be still, the cricket owns the talking stick.

In silence nestles the Goddess.

Truth belongs to no one, but us all.

Ode to Cujo

(died on June 18, 2018)

Two weeks postmortem, you appear
dream-climbing up a tall stump,
glowing, menacing, poised to pounce,
telling me your demise
veered from that which I surmised.

Actually, I found you unmarked but inert,
mere feet away from the crab-tree.
Your neck flopped when I cradled you.
I thought you fell and broke your neck.
I wept, buried you, and marked your grave.

After a trip, I gaped at tufts on the lawn,
you recycled to a wildcat wilderness?
Our bond was stronger than with any former pet –
fifteen years, three paintings, and thirty poems,
everlasting, your feisty and unique presence.

Your Litter House, food and water bowls
are *memento mori*, like your hypnotic glare:
Feed me and free me – inside or outdoors.
Your lap-time, nap-time, and precise preening,
larger than life, your absence howled for weeks.

But you meow, purr, in the full-contact wind.
And I have pensive confidence
what is Familiar is also now my very nature.

Awakening #1

Aghast at the Ghost of Christmas Past

Drinking in the blinking Santas and sleighs,
imbibing the twinkling doe and fawn,
I staggered through the neighbourhood
in the unseasonably warm night,
each Christmas light a blessing:

the mental ward didn't admit me;
my daughter safe with friends 'till I snapped to;
Time Magazines and slushy cocoa soothed my sleepless, sober
week;
red and green swaddled pines uplifted my eyes
to scope out sister lights, a stellar abundance.

White and blue sparkles appeased loneliness –
single after my star-crossed decade,
the cusp catalyzed my plea, "If the Eighties
are like the Seventies, help me or take me
now, God." The word Peace brightened a lawn.

I hugged my daughter home early, aghast
at her toppled world: farmed out at Christmas,
her dad scarpered, her mom trying to get locked up.
Rising to help her voice desolate dispossession, her puckish
frustration,
I missed my inching toward a widening star's reveal,
its magnitude yet to be unveiled.

(New Year's Eve, 1979)

The Other Side of the Desk

Neighbours plied me with the Twenty Questions
that spring of 1980
after my husband fled my nightmare headscape
where a dream of driving brakeless stalked my sleep.
My pusher psychiatrist pressed a clinic on me,
aware of my lies about imbibing
and my exploitation of suicidal despair.
She refused to buoy me through
the maelstrom of my venom-drizzling past.

The only show for the second session,
a twice-fired social worker, I glowered
at the petty-minded shrink and at the louts mesmerized
by the Queen Mother's highfalutin parade.
I told them what they could do with Queen Mum
and stomped out to my rust-bucket Dodge Dart.

In sloping Halifax, my neglected brakes went for broke
and I flew through red lights down Citadel Hill.
Ignoring the honks and finger waves –
at the crest of a slippery decline,
I turned the wrong way on a one-way street
and Social Services swerved me curbside.
I cried in wonder, "Just a bent license plate!;
God loves this miserable mock-up." Nightmare? Poof!

Unconditionally Heard

Short walks seemed Gold Medal worthy, ah hell,
throwing back the covers at all earned me the podium
in my divorced and diminished state.
I hired a helper to clean my split-level, totally detached,
and babbled my bizarre bio.

Shirley heard – she hugged me, did not damn me,
as I recounted eight dying, drunk
and cancer-struck, before I turned twenty-five,
words wafting on the wings of a Great Horned Owl.
She warmed to me as is, no guilt, no strings,

unlike childhood magpies modelling
how to scare off love, nesting self-pity.

Shirley's grace-filled acceptance fledged away
guilt, vague shame, but I still denied
my-last-one-standing guilt,
demon drink, though scary worry opened a chink.

(Late spring, 1980)

Awakening #4

A Clearing

Stumbling into Transcendental Meditation,
I stared at the prayer taped to my mentor's space.
Sanskrit floated in, bile out, twice daily, the purge.

Graced with a few hours
of unaided slumber, no booze, no balm,
bliss, natural sleep did exist,

caressing my defeated eyes, nerves
and neurons – slowly coming alive,
like Easter birthing smells in the air.

(Early June, 1980)

Awakening #5

Blessings Delivered

Normally not braving a visit to a friend's unknown
liquor supply, (yet still denying I'm a drunk),
my daughter and I winged west: I stole
my soon ex-friend's hidden hooch three times.

Attuned since June to my mantra, that July,
I opened my heart to the ether
topping Tunnel Mountain, and eased the fear
of my daughter's that she would fall off.

The pointedly infinite Rockies
overpowered my precociously Goth-suicidal self,
gifting me a lucid balm,
calming my seemingly necrotic neurons.

My irate hosts gave me *The Cracker Factory*
The word Hope shone on page nineteen,
later discovered no such word on that page!
Bottomed out, I divorced Barleycorn, god of booze,

and painstakingly overhauled
every nebulous thought and action –
transported to that galaxy-sized sober life,
shimmering magnitudes of gratitude.

[Only 8% of alcoholics stay sober.
Sober since July 19, 1980.]

Endnotes

8 – *Here's the Scoop, I'm a Thinker:*
> Greek philosopher, Demosthenes, orated better with a
> pebble-in-mouth practice.

26 – *Earth Lungs:*
> Diana Beresford-Kroeger, *Arboretum Borealis*, Ann
> Arbor: The University of Michigan Press, 2010.

30 – *Faerie Rings Bless:*
> *Go tabann* – suddenly, Gaelic.

31 – *Lower World Holds Power:*
> Working the *Twelve Steps* heals addictions and faulty
> living through self-honesty, atonement.
> *Barleycorn's Bar* – John Barleycorn is a nickname for
> the god of alcohol.

33 – *Georgian White Pine Dances:*
> "Big Lonely Doug" (Douglas Fir), Harley Rustad, *The
> Walrus,* October 2016.

36 – *Gabriel Is My Virgil:*
> Hoffman Quadrinity Process is held in Aurora,
> Ontario.
> *Divine Comedy,* Dante's guide Virgil.

40 – *Gabriel Glued Me Whole:*
> Athame – consecrated sword or wand used in healing
> Wicca rituals.
> Anagnorisis – the moment in a novel or play when a
> main character recognizes the true nature of another
> character.

45 – Forest *Supported Me:*
> Scethrog – Henry Vaughan's childhood cottage-size
> home in Welsh Brecon Beacons.
> Sunapee – lake and town in New Hampshire.

48 – *Ochre Epiphanies:*
> Scumbling – technique of dragging one or more layers
> of dry opaque paint over a bottom layer   that
> partially shows through the overlying layers.

49 – *Blow Cold Many Moons:*
> North Face – high tech outdoor wear.
> Sheila Watt-Cloutier, *The Right to be Cold,* Toronto:
> Penguin, 2015.
> Head of Intergovernmental Climate Change
> Committee's words of doom in first CBC airing.

51 – *Gumption Can't Suppress Arctic Breath:*
> *Samhain* – Celtic, Wicca, new year: celebrants honour
> the dead, vow to shed one bad trait.

58 – *Pagans Also Baptize:*
> Viper's Buglos, prickly weed with blue petals that fade
> to pink.

Acknowledgements:

Heartfelt thanks to Patti Welling for the idea of writing from Cujo's point of view, and to other friends/ supporters, Susan McCaslin, Penn Kemp, Kate Marshall Flaherty, Dave Bartlett, Charlotte Blair, Shelly Hazzard, and above all Sandra Harris, Peter Midgley and George Elliott Clarke.

Credits:

The poems below, some in earlier versions and titles, have
appeared in the following:

Canadian Woman Studies vol 32, #1, 2: *I Embrace
My Celtic Nature; Earth Care.*

The Prairie Journal, 2017: *Here's the Scoop; Sleeping
Solo, Sigh.*

The Bannister #31, 2016: *Encrypt Me Egyptian; Re:
Creativity, I Create Too.*

PoeArtry North, Third Place, Elana Wolff, Judge:
Ochre Epiphanies, poem and art.

Transitory Tango, Ronnie Brown, Editor: *I'm Also
Capsized; Interment.*

Heartwood Anthology, Leslie Strutt, Editor: 2018:
Beeches Quicken.

The Wishing Tree: *Earth Lungs, Georgian White
Pine Dances, Wilderness Chorale, Faerie Rings Bless.*

Phantom Parade: *Crone Intones, Interment.*

Parkland Poets Poem in Pocket: *Georgian White Pine
Dances.*

Permission to quote from John B. Lee's *Remains* and Albert
Moritz's *Sequence 115* graciously granted.

Publishing History: all books include my art.

We Are Malala, Inanna, 2019.

Dancing on a Pin, Inanna, 2015, long-listed for Lowther, part of IFOA's Battle of the Bards.

Class Acts, Inanna, 2013, in Kerry Clare's blog: Best Poetry Books of 2013.

Angelic Scintillations, Inanna, 2011, riffs off ancestor Henry Vaughan's *Silex Scintillans.*

Samsara: Canadian in Asia, Penn Kemp and Gavin Stairs, Pendas Productions, 2008.

Shaking Hands with the Night, Penn Kemp and Gavin Stairs, Pendas Productions, 2004.

Remyth, Cranberry Tree Press, 1997, as Kathy Fretwell.

Apple, Worm and All, Fiddlehead Poetry Books, 1979, as Kathy Tyler.

The Ultimate Contact, Fiddlehead Poetry Books, 1978, as Kathy Tyler.

Edited, Compiled, Illustrated books:

Intimate Passages, Beret Days Press, 2020.

The Eloquent She, Feminist Caucus Archives, League of Canadian Poets, 2006.

And no one knows the blood we share, Feminist Caucus Archives, LCP, 2005.